Smart Social Media

Your Guide To Becoming A Highly Paid Social Media Manager

Lasse Rouhiainen

ISBN-13: 978-1478129431
ISBN-10: 1478129433

What People Are Saying

"The strategies and techniques Lasse teaches in Smart Social Media work! I immediately applied what I learned to improve my own Facebook page & YouTube videos. Plus I now have another income stream as a Social Media Manager "

- Ronda Del Boccio, #1 Best Selling author and Celebrity Author Mentor www.profitablestorytelling.com

"If you are in a job transition looking for a new income opportunity or you currently help small businesses to improve the way they market then Smart Social Media is a must read book. After reading this book you will feel empowered and confident to offer marketing services to small businesses in such a way that you can earn a good income."

- James Kilgarriff, Peak Potential Coach for Harv Eker. www.jameskilgarriff.com

"This really is the 'go to' manual on social media, with practical and easy to understand action steps that anyone can apply to building a stronger online presence. So whether you are already a Social Media Manager or someone wanting to utilize powerful strategies to up-level your social media exposure, this is the book for you!"

- Sharon Worsley

Creator of the 4 Diamond Leadership System™ and author of 'The 4 Diamond Leader…How to Wake Up, Shake Up and Show Up in Business and Life' www.sharonworsley.com

Acknowledgments

I would like to thank my wife, Sandra, for her love and support. I would also like to thank my family, especially my parents, who have always been there for me.

I also would like to thank all of my clients and students, particularly the up-and-coming Social Media Managers, who willingly helped me to complete this book by answering a survey and sharing valuable information about their social media activities.

Annabel Lleonart, Arturo Valdivieso, Belen Bolivar, Carlos Londoño, Carmen Lopez, Carmen Sevilla, Daniel Rodriguez, Ebert Martinez, Fabián Herrera, Francisco Gomez, Harold Gutierrez, Hernan Iles, J.Ramón Risueño, José Castaño, Jose Tinedo, Laura Escudera, Luz Velasquez, Mariano Concha Cortés, Mathie López, Miriam Tabarez, Néstor Ávalos, Nubia Ulloa Abril, Pablino Jara, Paco Sala, Ricardo Rocha, Roberto Ibarra, Roberto Véliz, Santi Perdomo, Victor Rojas, Vladimir Veliz, Wilhelm Michael and all the other people on our Facebook group.

I would also like to extend my many thanks to the people who have helped me create this book. Ruben Gonzalez, for creating the book cover. Kristen Eckstein, for her great insights and tips regarding the cover design. And Ronda Del Boccio, for her support, advice, and encouragement to finish this book.

Finally, thanks to Alex Nghiem for inspiring me to complete this book and always sharing his valuable business knowledge.

Contents

Introduction

If you are an entrepreneur, online marketer, or business owner, you're probably aware that there are a great number of opportunities right now on the Internet in marketing or social media. However, most of them take too much time, money, or resources.

What if I could show you a proven system to quickly earn big money without the need for:

- A lot of traffic to your website
- Big list of subscribers
- Previous experience
- Large budget

Would you be interested?

The best part is that you can do this even if:

- You only have a handful of clients
- You don't enjoy selling
- You don't have technical skills

What I'm talking about is claiming your share of the current social media marketing boom and offering powerful and effective social media services to local companies in your area. It means getting paid and

1

providing real value to people who desperately need your help at the same time. In addition, you can create a profitable business without even doing most of the work!

I wrote this book because I wanted to encourage more people to start tapping into this great business opportunity. For the last three years, I have trained hundreds of small businesses in Europe and South America on YouTube and Facebook marketing. However, a large portion of small businesses are still somewhat clueless when it comes to using social media and are in need of help.

What has been the most fulfilling part for me is being able to see what the correct social media marketing can bring to businesses. However, there are many small business owners who don't have the time or knowledge to start implementing social media to their business, and so there exists a huge demand for people like you to help companies start promoting their products and services on Facebook and YouTube.

In this book, I refer to this line of work as "Social Media Manager," however don't get caught up in the name. The most important thing is the value you provide to your clients and, therefore, it's best to think of yourself as someone who helps local companies attract more clients through the use of social media.

In fact, as I explain later in this book, most companies will be more interested in working with you when you present yourself as an "online business consultant" or "social media consultant" because the title "consultant" is typically better received by companies. However, remember that the main thing is to provide valuable

2

services and help businesses find new customers using social media.

In the business world, sometimes the title Social Media Manager may refer to someone working on a company's payroll who manages their social media activities. However, in this book, the position refers exclusively to an independent consultant. Nevertheless, if you happen to work as a Social Media Manager for one company, you may still find valuable the information in this book when it comes to effectively running Facebook and YouTube - you may even get inspired to start your own profitable business.

In this hands-on guide, you will find strategies and techniques on how to implement social media for small and medium sizes businesses. However, some of the same strategies can be applied to bigger businesses too - which I have done myself while working with large banks and hotels.

In the last twelve months, I have been able to train more than 300 Social Media Managers and social media consultants and have included a section in this book where some of them share highly valuable tips with you. Their recommendations are based on real world experiences and so can greatly help those of you just getting started.

I have also been blessed to work with talented mentors and business strategy experts, and have included a section where they share tips on how to have a more profitable and solid Social Media Manager business.

This book was written primarily as a guide for my current mentoring students and, as such, I wanted to include as many points as possible. Therefore, in many chapters you won't find long paragraphs droning on about theoretical concepts. I have instead created numerous bullet lists of the most crucial action items so that you may use this book as a quick reference guide while implementing social media for your clients, without getting bogged down in unnecessary chatter.

My final recommendation to you is that you implement these strategies and techniques as soon as possible, because that is the only way you will achieve results.

To help you get started quickly, I have included special bonus resources for you the reader, including video tutorials, checklists, and templates.

Watch my quick video and claim your bonuses for free at:

www.smartsocialmedia.biz/vip

Let's get started since the clients are waiting for you...

Small Businesses Are Struggling and They Need Your Help

You can probably relate with many of the problems and challenges I hear my students mention during the various workshops and trainings I give on video marketing and social media marketing.

- "Internet marketing is too confusing and time-consuming."

- "I don't know how to build a big list or generate a lot of traffic on my website."

- "I don't have enough time to create my product and earn money online."

Most people who want to earn money online feel confused over everything that needs to be done in order to achieve success, including creating a product, building a list, contacting affiliates, etc.

The good news is that there is a better, simpler, and easier way of making money, and it's something you can do without having a university degree, previous experience, or technical skills. I'm referring to helping local companies who already have established products and services, but who don't know how to promote them online using social media!

As you might already know, traditional marketing channels like radio, TV, and newspapers have become ineffective. The majority of consumers now use online media to research for comments and opinions about products and services.

Sites like Facebook.com, YouTube, and Google.com have become important platforms for local businesses to satisfy this online demand for information. With these and other researching and advertising services, consumers can easily find out more about specific products and services through consumer comments and videos reviewing the products they are interested in buying.

However, most local companies don't have the necessary knowledge to take advantage of these new marketing strategies, and they are willing to pay someone like you who can help them.

In addition, this job is fun, exciting, and develops skills for an increasingly demanding field as the importance of social media grows bigger and bigger each year.

The biggest concern I hear from my coaching and mentoring clients is that social media is too complicated and overwhelming - that there are too many sites, platforms, strategies, and tools to keep track of and stay familiarized with. I always recommend that they ask themselves: "How can I create the most value for my customers so that they will want to keep paying me month after month?"

The answer is quite simple. In the beginning, focus on YouTube and Facebook marketing. These two sites are adequate for producing quick results for your clients.

Later on, you can help them develop marketing through Twitter, Linkedin, and Google Plus, by creating a compelling presence on those sites and adding their business to "Google Plus Local" (previously Google Places) along with several local directories. These strategies and tools will be discussed later in the book.

In addition to delivering Facebook and YouTube marketing, as a Social Media Manager you will need to discover the fine art of getting clients. Often times, this is simpler than most people think because the services offered are very specialized and in high demand. At the end of this book, I have included a chapter discussing some of the most effective strategies for finding your first clients, including those used by my current students.

Perhaps the most important task when just beginning is figuring out the ideal audience for your client, along with the primary product to be promoted. I normally survey my clients first to really understand their business and be better able to help them.

Knowing how to effectively use Facebook and YouTube to attract new customers is key. Nevertheless, it's equally if not more important to also maintain an open line of communication with your clients. Your client is your product and you need to know what they want, how they are feeling, if you are to provide your best and most effective services. Open, two-way communication is the only way to achieve this.

In this book, you will get a clear understanding on how to manage Facebook pages for your future clients. However, some of my students also find benefits in teaching their clients to update and create Facebook content themselves. This way companies will learn how to do the content creation part themselves and so will focus on monitoring the process and creating a strategy.

This method is fantastic as it helps you to save time. By not having to create new content all of the time for every company, you can focus more on monitoring and making sure they are doing the right things. Plus, you can always sell them more consulting hours if they want to learn more.

In summary, becoming a Social Media Manager or online business consultant only requires familiarizing yourself with a few simple strategies in obtaining new clients, delivering YouTube and Facebook marketing, outsourcing work, and offering additional services. All of these topics are covered in this book in a practical, easy-to-apply manner.

How You Can Earn Money as a Social Media Manager

Some small and medium-sized businesses already know the importance of conducting social media marketing with sites like YouTube and Facebook. However, many small business owners are very busy and don't have the time needed. These owners are instead eager to pay someone else who can provide these social media services for them.

Here are some of the main reasons why business owners can't do social media marketing for themselves:

- They don't have time.
- They don't know how to create high-definition videos.
- They think there is a lot of technical skill needed.

You might be wondering, "why don't small businesses hire big advertising agencies to help with social media?" The answer is that these agencies focus on huge multinational corporations, not on small local businesses. This creates a large demand for what I call "local Social Media Managers" who can help small businesses by creating their YouTube channel, shooting videos for them, and optimizing these marketing tools for the best results and also delivering effective Facebook marketing for them.

Which local businesses most need social media marketing?

My coaching clients and I have helped local businesses of all kinds to find clients. Here is a list of some local businesses in your area that might need help with video marketing:

- Dentists
- Lawyers
- Restaurants
- Accountants
- Real Estate agents
- Chiropractors
- Travel agents
- Physical Therapists

However, don't limit yourself to companies in these sectors. Practically all kinds of companies need social media to succeed today. Most of these companies struggle with creating social media or video marketing and need someone like you to help them generate leads and improve their presence online.

I see a rapidly growing demand for people and companies who can help small businesses with their social media efforts. I have seen all kinds of traditional businesses like newspapers and accounting firms, for example, create social media departments, recognizing it's a great opportunity.

The market for this work is huge right now and you have a chance to claim your share of this social media boom. This book was written to lay out a step-by-step guide on this new field so that you can provide a more professional and effective service.

As with all new things, you might be scared to begin offering your services to local companies. However, understand that having doubts and being scared is a natural part of the process of growing and starting something new.

When I obtained my first client, I too had many doubts of my ability to deliver, but I took action, got excited about being able to help my client, and knew that I could learn as I went along.

Also, accept the fact that you don't have to be perfect when you're just beginning. You just have to get going and start building experience with setting up Facebook pages or creating simple videos for companies. I normally recommend starting with a friend's business, someone you already know and are comfortable with, just to see how easy it is and improve your confidence in your ability to do this.

One of my mentors, Tom Beal, said, "You don't have to get it right, you just have to get going." Those words have helped me tremendously when starting many exciting and challenging projects, including writing this book.

The opportunity to build a big and successful business by helping small businesses grow is huge right now. But, you have to get in early, now, before there is more competition. That you may have doubts is fine, however, you need to just accept that you will always feel this way about taking big steps and get over your fears - act now.

Powerful Insights from Social Media Managers

Just before this book went to printing I conducted a survey with some of my Social Media Manager coaching clients, asking questions like, "what do you like most about being a Social Media Manager" and "what mistakes should a new Social Media Manager avoid?"

The following is a summary of answers from people currently working as Social Media Managers from nine different countries. These summaries convey a very powerful list of things you should learn in order to achieve success as a Social Media Manager.

Question 1: What do you like most about being a Social Media Manager and being able to offer marketing services to local businesses?

- "It's great to be part of a new era in marketing (social media marketing), transforming society and the way companies do business."

- "What I like most is being able to work from home, my own way, and having the ability to get customers through the Internet anywhere in the world."

- "What I like most is that it is a profession that will give me the financial freedom I have long sought, and allows me to choose my own hours; I have total freedom of my life."

- "The personal branding is what I like best, because customers trust you more and will start to seek you out."

- "What I love most about my job is that I am in contact with various communities and I have the opportunity to get to know them, know their necessities, preferences, and in return they get all that I can offer. There is high demand in social media and there will always be more opportunities."

- "I like to interact with entrepreneurs in all types of businesses, and offer opportunities to increase their earnings and improve their presence on the Internet. That is something companies like very much."

- "I really enjoy showing the benefits that social media brings to local businesses and see the "Wow" expression on peoples' faces who didn't know that this can be done. Also, contributing to the growth of their business, being part of the planning, and going step by step in the growth of entrepreneurs regarding the use of social networks in their business."

- "What I like is that you're selling an intangible product, but still something real, which allows you to see results in the real world every day.

Actually, we are helping local businesses and others during this global financial crisis, and all the help they can get is much appreciated. Many companies do not have the time or knowledge to do social media marketing themselves, so our work is very important for them."

Question 2: Please share some "mistakes to avoid" for those just beginning:

- "One error is that new Social Media Managers do not know how to plan ahead. To be successful, it is crucial that a plan be formulated and set in place; you cannot function without one. You have to be professional and, for this reason, it is important to be prepared for the work that you want to achieve. "

- "Common mistake is not having any plan for monitoring service proposals sent to clients. You should have a system to register to whom you sent proposals. "

- "A frequent mistake is a lack of perseverance. If you intend to publish something today, but nothing in the week to follow, it is better not to publish anything at all. This work does not consist solely of submitting photos. Rather, it requires a consistent stream of material in order to bring profits to the business that hired you. "

- "Do not force social networks on uninterested clients. It is better to first create a relationship with the business, gain their confidence, and then show them the results and benefits of using your services as a Social Media Manager. "

- "It is important to communicate clearly. Social Media Managers must know when and how to speak, and when to avoid talking too much. By being selective and critical in communications, you avoid offering too much information that may be used against you or scare away the client."

- "Do not promise what you cannot deliver. Also, be clear about deadlines and monitoring that will be done for your clients. Occasionally, you might offer services that cannot be completed due to unforeseen time constraints or lack of information. This problem is very common and leaves the client disappointed. "

- "Avoid offering all services to everyone. You have to define your niche or sector in the market. Specialize in a particular sector where you know its needs and work with clients needing those services. "

- "Study and analyze the sector or businesses for which you are offering your services. You need to know both the businesses and the products that they offer. Try to socialize, not sell. Have in mind the objectives of the business so that you will know which type of social network is best for promoting their brand or products. Once you have determined this, create your plan for success. "

- "Payment is important. Do not randomly charge for your work. Define prices ahead of time and be clear with your clients about amounts and payment dates. This is how you are earning your living, so you should spend some time elaborating on your plan for it. "

- "Time is money, so here is a schedule for you: Planning 15%-Education 35%-Action 50%."

- "Another common mistake is not to value the work that you are doing. You have to believe in what you are doing and appreciate it. Begin to value yourself. As difficult as it seems, if you can do this, you will value your work. "

- "Social Media Managers have the task of informing clients and measuring the results. If you do not measure what you are doing or with the appropriate tools, you will not be able to see your achievements and progress. If you do not have quantifiable data to show your clients, eventually your client will no longer desire your services. "

- "Another thing to avoid is bringing your home problems to work. That is to say, when you are acting as a Social Media Manager and working in social networks, do not talk about yourself or private issues. Keep conversations focused on your client's business. You have the obligation of making a name for yourself and watching your online reputation. If you are having a bad day, do not take it out on a client and/or fan, etc. Always remember that you need to respond to your clients' needs, not your own. "

- "Make sure to determine the number of clients you are capable of serving at any one time. Do not take on more work that you can handle. It is advisable that you define a set period of time that you can dedicate to the needs of each client. "

Tips From Business Strategy Experts

I have also been blessed to work with talented mentors and business strategy experts, and in this chapter they share tips on how to have a more profitable and solid Social Media Manager business.

"Set up effective communication system with your clients"

"Educate your client on how to communicate with you. Establish strong communication with your new clients and then later set the limits. If you give all of your client's full access to your time, it can quickly become a nightmare when you have several clients wanting to contact you all day long. We have systems in place like a knowledge database where clients can submit tickets and get their answer immediately. We give monthly reports to the clients and they get 1 or 2 calls, depending on the package they buy from us."

Shahar Boyayan, Owner and Founder of buzzbooster.com

"How to raise your fees"

"After you have some experience serving others with your products and/or services, and they feel good about what they've received at the time, I'd recommend that you make every attempt to capture their excitement (testimonials, photos, video, etc.) and consider raising your rates for future prospects.

You are only worth the combination of (1) what you have the courage to ask for and (2) what potential clients see value in (for themselves) and are willing to pay you for those benefits.

Always test raising your rates. With more profit, you can afford to live an improved life of fun and excitement that, in turn, is what really attracts others. At the end of the day, that's all they really want too. "

Rob Canyon, Business Strategy Consultant, robcanyon.com

"Focus your services on only one sector or industry"

"If I would have to start all over again, one thing I would do differently would be to "go deep instead of wide," meaning I would focus my marketing services on one particular industry. Turn your first client into your biggest fan and then ask them for a video testimonial. Then, with that testimonial, go to another business in the same industry (in another location) that knows your first client.

When they see the amazing testimonial, they will jump at the opportunity to work with you. Let them know that you only work with one person in any particular industry and location. An additional benefit is that you will start to know their lingo and business really well and helping them will become second nature. "

David Preston, Founder of Legendary Consultants Group offlinegoldmine.com/warchest

"How To Charge Top Dollars"

"Always focus on the benefits, not the mechanics, when you speak with business owners. What they want is more free time with their loved ones, more sales, and higher profits.

To be able to charge top-dollar, align what you offer with what they want and communicate strategic value. Speak in terms of the benefits and outcomes they want, not on what you do. A business owner will pay far more for a way to stay in touch with their customers than for a website or fan page.

Alex Nghiem, Business Strategist & Trainer to Consultants www.expertriches.tv

"The Follow Your Money Strategy For Getting New Clients"

"The best and fastest way to get started in offering your services as a Social Media Manager is to use the "Follow Your Money" strategy. In other words, go to the small businesses in your area where you already spend money on a regular basis. You know, your favorite restaurant, the hair salon, your dentist, etc, and ask to talk with the owners about their social media strategy.

Chances are they don't have one, and that will open the door for you to become their "trusted advisor" on Facebook, YouTube, Twitter, Linkedin, etc. This is a simple, yet powerful strategy when you are just getting started, because these business owners already know you, and they feel a certain level of obligation to speak with you because your are "their client".

In other words, they need you as much as you need them. So go ahead, start "Following Your Money," and before you know it you will have 3 to 5 clients who will happily pay you on a monthly basis to manage their social media presence. "

Charles Denney, The Online Persuasionist, Webpresario.com

Introduction to Facebook Marketing

Currently, Facebook is the largest and arguably the most important social networking site in the world, bringing together all sorts of people, businesses, and organizations. Facebook has nearly one billion users worldwide, offering numerous opportunities for both small and medium size companies to interact, communicate, and engage with potential customers.

According to official Facebook statistics, the average user logs 55 minutes daily on their website, with more than 350 million active users accessing Facebook through their mobile devices. For more on Facebook statistics you can visit their official page at www.facebook.com/press/info.php?statistics.

For many local businesses, their Facebook page is becoming more important Internet property than their traditional website. Facebook offers a reliable, easily accessible forum where consumers can leave comments on a company's product, interact and share photos, and easily recommend the company to their friends. Most small business owners have begun to understand the great power of Facebook marketing, however, most are normally too busy to implement Facebook marketing for themselves; they find it very time consuming and confusing. This has created a great demand for Social Media Managers.

Some benefits that having a Facebook page offers to companies includes:

- From the point of view of a small local business, Facebook pages are far easier to upload and post fresh content than traditional websites. You can also update a Facebook page from a mobile phone.

- From the customer's point of view, a Facebook page is much safer, and more interesting and exciting to visit than the traditional company website because they give customers the possibility to interact and engage.

- Companies can convey their story by sharing photos and information of their products. An example of this is Facebook's Timeline that enables companies to express their unique identity with features like a cover photo - an attractive image at the top of their Facebook page. This cover image can be changed at any time.

- Facebook pages can incorporate advertising through Facebook ads, targeting specific demographics of consumers according to their age, location, and interests.

- One of the main benefits of having a Facebook page is being able to create an active community around a company's products or services.

- Facebook pages serve as a powerful tool for asking questions or conducting surveys among the customers.

- Facebook pages enable consumers to send messages directly to companies, enabling better communication because so many consumers now prefer Facebook messaging over emails.

- Facebook provides extensive statistics to track the age and location of people who visit your page, and other important insights like what day of the week people most visit, etc.

- Companies can share unique offers and discounts that customers can then print or present in-store on their mobile phone.

- Facebook pages rank highly among Google search results. Further, any content included on one's page is also available to people without Facebook accounts.

As a Social Media Manager, your primary task will be to create and manage Facebook pages for your clients. There is no limit on how many pages you can manage - across multiple clients, or several pages for a single client. For instance, a store selling chocolate desserts could have one Facebook page in their name and another one related to their product, like "people who love chocolate desserts." However, I recommend building one page well before opening other pages.

Clients can be any kind of local business, ranging from

restaurants, to gyms, beauty salons, local stores, accounting firms, and so forth. On the section ¨ Facebook Marketing Step 4: Creating Your Action Plan¨ I will share step-by-step the plan you should implement when you do Facebook marketing for small businesses.

Facebook Marketing Step 1: Creating a Content Plan

The main element for a successful Facebook page is publishing interesting, educational, and entertaining content. There are different types of content that you can post on Facebook pages, such as videos, photos, quizzes, questions, announcements, offers, status updates, and generic news.

Most small and medium size companies are clueless on how to create a powerful content plan. As a Social Media Manager, one of your main tasks is to create a content plan for the first 30 days in getting the Facebook page started. I recommend using an Excel spreadsheet to help organize the plan.

You should have ongoing meetings with your clients and talk about future content to be published on Facebook. This will help you get ideas from them and to publish important announcements.

Some companies have "content idea banks" where pre-written Facebook posts and updates are kept. This allows them to quickly access use the information whenever necessary.

Create a content plan

Before creating a content plan, I recommend you get to know your client and their business very well. I always suggest to my students that they send out a survey to companies to find out what is unique about that particular organization and how they stand apart from their competitors. In addition, you will want to understand who your client's ideal customer demographics are - age, location, and special interests like hobbies, etc. This will help you to create authentic and engaging content to form the cornerstone of their page.

You can meet with your client on a weekly or bi-monthly basis to discuss fresh and exclusive content, as well as to brainstorm on future material for the page. Normally, fans like to see "behind the scenes content," for example, a restaurant showing videos or photos from their kitchen - areas that clients typically cannot access. When it comes to content itself, I recommend always having a chatty and informal tone because customers want to see that there is a "human touch" - that the page is managed by authentic people who really care about their Facebook fans.

One of the special features on any Facebook page is the ability to post for a specific, targeted audience. Next time you are posting on Facebook, check out the dropdown menu next to the button labeled "post". This section allows you to specify posts to a particular audience according to their language and location; this content will not be seen by any other fans of the page. This is a quite useful feature, especially for pages with a large audience.

The following is a list suggestions on where to get content:

- FAQ's by the company's current customers. For example, a hotel should ask the reception manager to gather all of the main questions and inquiries of the previous 60 days. Then, educational content would be created on the basis of these questions and published on the Facebook page.

- Videos created by the company.

- Interesting, educational, and inspirational videos on YouTube can also be used and shared on the Facebook page.

- Publishing interesting and unique photos is recommended. Ask for all of the photos that the company currently has, and then get them to take new photos on their smartphones for quick sharing on Facebook.

- Share content on current events. For example, a flower store can share recommendations for which kinds of flowers to buy your loved one on Valentine's Day.

- Have updates that don't have anything to do with your products or services. Remember, people are on Facebook to spend their time and communicate socially with each other. Therefore, it's recommended to post updates like "Happy Monday" to encourage people to start their weeks with energy, or inquire into people's weekend plans. This kind of communication is very innocent and non-confrontational. Keeping a friendly relationship will help to build a community and improve trust with the page's followers.

- Every now and then, the company can create contests on Facebook. However, because Facebook is constantly changing the rules for using contests, if you decide to do so it's recommended that you first review the rules for promoting on Facebook here: www.facebook.com/promotions_guidelines.php, or use some professional Facebook applications such as Easypromosapp.com, Strutta.com or Wildfireapp.com

- While managing the Facebook page, monitor who the most active followers are and who always comments or participates in discussions. These people can be very valuable for the company, and it's nice to get to know them better by talking on phone or giving them some responsibility.

Facebook Marketing Step 2:
Increasing Engagement

One of the primary habits one must obtain for managing a successful Facebook page is the constant encouragement for interaction and participation.

Some companies consider Facebook and other social networks to be like a bulletin board, where they can overwhelm the public with constant announcements. Smart marketers, however, understand the value of precise engagements with their fans. This means, rather than flooding pages with company posts, to encourage user participation. From the customer's perspective, this type of communication is far more interesting and enriching than passive observance of a company's ads.

Some of the most engaging content on Facebook tends to be colorful photos, or photos where you ask people to write captions. Every now and then, it's important to ask "fill in the blank" questions where the fans are asked to provide the content. For example, a restaurant could ask, "<fill in the blank> is my favorite food". Facebook users love this kind of question because it allows them to share what is important to them.

One of the most interactive Facebook pages is Zappos, located at www.facebook.com/zappos. Take a few days to browse their page, see what kind of posts they are making, and how they encourage participation. On my own Facebook community, I sometimes ask non-business related questions such as, "It's Friday, what are your plans for this weekend"? People love this because it creates a sense of community and makes them feel special; it shows you care about them and are not just trying to sell something. Consequently, this enables companies to know their followers better, allowing them to collaborate in creating a powerful community.

The primary purpose of increasing engagement is to create a sense of community and to show the fans that the page is all about them - not about the company. You should always encourage participation and reward the most active fans. Public recognition is a great way to do this.

According to a research published by Buddy Media, here are some guidelines on how to make engaging posts on your Facebook page:

- Avoid writing very long posts. Most people do not have the time to read lengthy segments. Keep the length of your post to 80 characters or less.

- Do not use "url" shortening services, like https://bitly.com/

- When you have important announcements, post them on either a Thursday or Friday. Engagement rates on Thursdays and Fridays are 18% higher than other days of the week.

- Use action keywords when posting and have them written down somewhere visible in your office. According to this study, some of the best words to use are "like, take, submit, watch, post, comment, tell us, and check."

- Always end your post with a question. Posts with questions at the end tend to have a 15% higher engagement rate.

- Use interrogative keywords: "where, when, would and should." These promote the highest engagement rates.

These findings can be found on the study by Buddy Media called "Strategies for Effective Facebook Wall Posts: a Statistical Review".

Facebook Marketing Step 3: Creating a Promotional Plan

Some companies have the attitude of "let's just build a Facebook page and everyone will find it." However, simply building a Facebook page does not get you very far; you also have to create a plan to promote it.

Be creative. Try to come up with different ways for getting people to visit the Facebook page and, more importantly, click the "like" button.

This chapter is divided into two sections, offline and online promotion. Each provides action items you can implement immediately.

Some companies who open a Facebook page only focus on promoting it to get new customers. However, having a Facebook page can be a very powerful tool to share company news with current clients and facilitate communication and discussion.

Therefore, especially when working with companies who have a physical location, focus your attention on creating different strategies to get the current customers to join the Facebook page, build loyalty, and generate repeated business.

Basic steps for promoting Facebook pages online

One of the fastest ways to promote Facebook pages online is by using Facebook ads and posting relevant, engaging, and fun content. Here is a short list of ideas on how to promote Facebook pages online:

- Get the company's employees to share the Facebook page url on their personal Facebook profile and to mention it to all of their contacts.

- Include a Facebook page "Like Box" on your client's website - you can generate the necessary code to do so at: https://developers.facebook.com/docs/reference/plugins/like-box/

- Write a blog post about the Facebook page on the company's website. Also, every time you have something interesting happening on the Facebook page, like a survey or competition, write a blog post about it and also promote it on Twitter and YouTube.

- You may also test Facebook advertising and design a small starting budget to experiment with it. Facebook advertising will be discussed more in depth later in this book.

- Mention the Facebook page address on YouTube and any other social media sites you manage.

- One of your main jobs is to reserve the client a username for their Facebook page so that the various offline promotional strategies may be implemented as soon as possible. User names can be reserved at the following site: www.facebook.com/username.

Steps for promoting Facebook pages offline:

- Use the Facebook page's "url" in all of the client company's email signatures.

- Include the "url" in all print materials that the company may distribute, such as flyers and catalogues.

- Display the "url" prominently inside of your store so that visitors will see it clearly. Remember to offer incentives for people who join the Facebook page, such as a restaurant offering free dessert.

- Remind employees to make promotion of the Facebook page a priority. Encourage people to 'like' it and become 'fans' of the page.

- Instruct your clients' employees to mention the page to all of the company's clients, either in person or on the phone.

Facebook Marketing Step 4: Creating Your Action Plan

In order to successfully create and manage a Facebook page for a company, you need a clear step-by-step action plan. In this section, I share a generic plan that will get you started, however, you can customize it according to your client's needs. This plan is divided into the following sections for an easier read: planning, content, and promoting.

Planning:

- Talk with your client and define goals for their Facebook page. For example, a local restaurant's goal could be to use the page to better connect with their current and future clients, and to share exclusive deals and fresh content (such as photos, videos, and news about their business). It's crucial for your client and long-term work together that from the beginning they have a clear understanding of the purpose of their page.

- Get to know your client and their products well. Send them a survey with detailed questions like, "what are your main products," "what sets you apart from your competition," etc. The more you know about your client, the more success you will have in managing their page.

- Define the ideal customer targeted to "like" the page. Be clear on geographical location, age, hobbies, gender, etc.

- Identify companies to serve as a benchmark; learn from them. There are a lot of businesses that have excelled at posting engaging content and creating a strong community among their Facebook fans. Zappos is a model example of the brand I like to learn from, located at Facebook.com/zappos and Starbucks at Facebook.com/starbucks. Try to find two or three companies that engage in great Facebook marketing and visit their pages frequently. Make notes on what you find most interesting.

- Ask your client to send you all of their photos, or visit them and take your own that can be used on Facebook. You can also later edit these photos using online tools, such as http://pixlr.com/editor/ and www.picmonkey.com

- Brainstorm on some incentives that can be offered to people who click on "Like". People love deals and discounts, and using these tools is a great way to encourage Facebook users to visit the business's page. For example, a restaurant could give a free dessert for people who show one code they have printed off of Facebook. Also consider, what kind of time-sensitive deals could be given away.

- Schedule time to update your client's Facebook page. Normally, it's recommended that you do it once in the morning and once again in the evening, depending on how many fans the page has. You should also set aside time every two weeks to analyze the Facebook page insights for all your clients and send each of them a summary of the results.

- Figure out how your client wishes to response to negative comments. Don't be afraid of negative comments. Instead, use them to grow and improve upon the page. Always respond publicly and openly first to all negative feedback and never argue with people. Then, try to move the conversation offline by contacting the person and speaking on the phone with him or her.

Content:

- Review the section on creating a content plan and fill in a spreadsheet with all of the possible page content for the first 10 to 30 days (photos, videos, questions, etc.). This will provide clarity and also allow you to post content quickly when managing several sites concurrently.

- Create weekly features. For example, one of my clients has a Facebook page on Rabbit Hutches (www.facebook.com/TheRabbitHutchShop) on which, every Friday, they share funny pictures of rabbits. This has helped them tremendously to increase community participation on their Facebook page.

- Creation of the page: - Go to www.facebook.com/pages/create.php and follow the simple step-by-step instructions on how to create your client's page.

- Create a cover and profile image for your client's site. According to the new Facebook Timeline rules, the cover image cannot include call to actions, a phone number, or the business's physical address. For examples of some attractive cover images, please visit this book's resource page at www.smartsocialmedia.biz/vip.

- Once the page has its first followers, you can go to www.facebook.com/username and select a unique username for access to the page. This will establish a web address that can be inserted into all of the company's marketing materials.

- Fill in the information on the "about" section, including your client's telephone number and physical address. - Add apps to the page. I recommend using some big Facebook app companies, like www.wildfireapp.com or www.involver.com/applications. These sites in particular offer a large selection of very useful apps.

- Add some of the company's employees to assist as site administrators. This is important because, if something were to happen to your account and you couldn't access Facebook, the page would still be accessible and managed.

- If you use a smartphone such as the iPhone, test updating the page. If you are able, this will help you to update Facebook pages on the go and can save you a lot of time down the road.

Promotion:

- Review the section called "Facebook promotion plan" and make a list of all of the main action points you will implement.

- You should also consider whether you will be using Facebook ads, which we talk about in more depth in the following section.

These are some basic steps for successfully starting to manage a Facebook page. However, you should always customize this plan according to a particular client's needs. In addition, remember that managing Facebook pages is a fun and exciting job. You should do it a in way that makes you comfortable. Sometimes local companies will want you to create and manage the page for the first few weeks before training them to manage it for themselves. This sort of training is also a good service for Social Media Managers to offer and, in general, you can earn a lot from providing this to companies.

www.smartsocialmedia.biz/vip

Facebook Advertising Tips

Any business can create advertisements promoting their Facebook page or website. Facebook ads offer one of the most powerful forms of paid adverting on the Internet, although it will take some time and effort to learn how to use them correctly. The biggest benefits of Facebook advertising are that it's based on demographics and that you can target people based on their hobbies and interest.

For example, a women's fitness club in Miami could target their ads to women who live in Miami and, in their Facebook profile, indicate that they like fitness and wellness. This type of advertising is very cost effective and helps the company quickly improve their awareness among the local community. Consequently, Facebook advertising is one of the most effective ways to quickly increase the number of fans for one Facebook page. As a Social Media Manager, you can design part of your fee to cover Facebook advertising, allowing them to expediently increase the number of targeted fans. Before starting, you should carefully read Facebook's guidelines for advertising which establish how to create ads in compliance with their advertising rules - located at www.facebook.com/ad_guidelines.php

The key steps for properly beginning with Facebook ads include: designing your ad, identifying your target market, deciding on your budget, and periodically monitoring and reviewing your ad performance. I recommend designating $40 USD to promote your first Facebook page just to discover how powerful Facebook ads can be for your business.

Let's now discuss the main steps involved in creating your first Facebook ads. These tips are divided into the following sections: generic tips, designing your ad, targeting, and deciding on your budget. These are the main topics you will need to tackle when beginning to promote with Facebook ads and understanding each section will help you to create more effective advertising campaigns.

The following is a list of key recommendations for running an effective advertising campaign on Facebook.

• **Generic tip:** Create a specific goal for your campaign, such as promoting time sensitive offers for a small business. It's recommended that you include the company's phone number and location in the ad to allow for the possibility of direct contact by the public.

• **Generic tip:** The performance of Facebook ads normally decreases over time because they are showed to the same target market over and over again. Therefore, be ready to make small changes every now and then to revitalize their effectiveness.

• **Designing your ad:** Your company image is perhaps the most important element of an ad campaign. Take the time to find and edit compelling images. You can use some online image editors such as http://pixlr.com/editor/. When selecting an image, use colors that stand out from the normal Facebook scheme (blue and white). Spend one week monitoring your own

Facebook account and analyze the Facebook ads you find drawing your attention - save them so that you can model them later on.

• **Designing your ad:** Designing an image that captures people's attention is vital to the success of your campaign. Try to use eye-catching emotional images of faces because people on Facebook are conditioned to seeing photos of people.

• **Designing your ad:** For the title of your ad you can test using questions, they normally convert better than other kind of titles. Avoid doing ads like "Hi, please like our Facebook page". Instead, offer something more specific for people who visit your Facebook page.

• **Targeting:** Specify the target audiences for your ads. Ask your client what their typical customer demographics is, including age, gender, hobbies, and geographical location. The more specific the targeting, the more effective the advertising will be.

• **Targeting:** Once your Facebook page starts to attract activity, you can visit 'Page Insights' to discover the age and locations of those fans interacting the most with it. Then, you can create ads that specifically target that market.

• **Deciding on your budget:** After selecting your target market, Facebook will automatically propose a "suggested bid". This is not the amount you will pay, it is the maximum amount you are willing to pay. When just starting out, it's recommended that you set aside an amount slightly lower than the Facebook suggestion. For example, if the suggested Facebook amount is $0.35 USD, you can set it to $0.30 USD instead.

• **Deciding on your budget:** You need to decide on your daily budget for the ad campaigning. When just beginning the process, you can keep it down - for example, to $5 USD.

• **Monitor and review:** Create different variations of your ad so that you can test different images or variations of text. See which one brings the best results.

• **Monitor and review:** Frequently visit your ads at www.facebook.com/ads/manage to monitor and analyze your campaigns. Run your Facebook ads for one to two weeks. After this period, make minor adjustments to your ads and target segments.

Facebook Marketing Case Study - Entremares Hotel

One of my first marketing clients as a Social Media Manager was the Entremares Hotel in La Manga de Mar Menor in Murcia, Spain. One of the key factors that has helped Entremares to achieve success both on YouTube and Facebook is that the company's management believes in social media and, therefore, decided to invest in its use to promote their businesses. The owner of Entremares Hotel, Alberto Inglés, share his opinion with us:

"Facebook marketing has helped us to create a large community of followers. Our Facebook page now has more than 20,000 fans who interact with us and share information with new customers staying at the hotel. We are pleased to invest in Facebook advertising; I consider it more effective and profitable than Google Adwords advertising."

"Having seen first-hand just how much customers enjoy using Facebook to get to know our company, this summer (2012) we will be introducing three new initiatives to allow our many Facebook fans to meet and interact with our employees offline. For starters, we will be incorporating a new Facebook fan office at Entremares to assist fans visiting us. Additionally, we will be implementing a physical Facebook wall where people can write what they like about the Hotel. Last but not least, we will be instituting a photo screen with QR codes. These innovative proposals will set us apart from the competition and provide customers with a unique experience they will be sure to remember."

You can find the Entremares Facebook page at www.facebook.com/hotelentremares and their YouTube channel at www.youtube.com/entremareslamanga

Introduction to Video Marketing

Video marketing is one of the most effective marketing methods used today because it helps companies to not only sell more product, but also to build credibility and trust with prospective clients.

Local companies have a huge opportunity to leverage the power of video marketing. It is new enough that not many companies have begun implementing its use, but is catching on as an extremely useful tactic for showing their human side. Connecting with customers in this way is important because potential clientele want to see the company's staff before buying a product, visiting a shop, or eating at a restaurant.

Here are just a few of the amazing statistics about video marketing when it comes to local companies:

- "Online videos are 53 times more likely to get a first-page Google ranking than a text page." - Forrester Research Study.

- "56% of advertisers surveyed view online video advertising as "more effective" than other forms of advertising." - BrightRoll Survey of Advertising Industry.

- "Over 3 billion videos are viewed per day on YouTube, and more video is uploaded to YouTube in one month than the 3 major US networks created in 60 years." – Source: YouTube.

- "500 years of YouTube video are watched every day on Facebook, and over 700 YouTube videos are shared on Twitter each minute." Source: YouTube.

- "100 million people take a social action on YouTube (likes, shares, comments, etc.) every week" Source: YouTube.

- "Internet video will account for 57% of all consumer Internet traffic in 2014." Cisco Systems' Visual Networking Index Forecast.

One of the greatest benefits of video marketing is that it can help local businesses rank on the first page of a Google search. Since Google owns YouTube, YouTube videos can improve a company's presence in a consumer's online researching well if certain keywords are used. One example of this would be titling a video for a local Italian restaurant located in Dallas, Texas as "Italian restaurant in Dallas."

Video marketing will provide your client with more exposure and leads, and will also help their brand recognition. Ideally, each of your clients should have at least 10 videos on YouTube. Consumers today are very demanding and prefer to review all kinds of content before making a decision on their purchase. The first of your client's videos could include testimonials, interviews where the employees share valuable content, tutorials where viewers will learn something valuable, and so on.

www.smartsocialmedia.biz/vip

Video Marketing Step 1: Planning

Planning is fundamental for every successful video marketing campaign. It is essential to dedicate some time to the planning phase to solidify your aims for the overall project and determine what will be need to accomplish your goals.

Before creating the videos, you will need to know some basic information about your client; for example, who will be their target customer, what will be the main product they want to promote, etc. Don't overcomplicate this step - you will only need to obtain basic information.

Focus on creating short videos

The best way for a company to begin video marketing is by concentrating on producing short videos. The majority of small and medium-sized companies successfully using YouTube have done so by filming videos lasting no longer than two minutes, often less. Plus, you will save a lot of time when you keep your videos short.

Some reasons why short videos are more appropriate:

- Consumers have a short attention span. Often, they will not watch longer YouTube videos to the end.

- It is quicker and easier to create a large number of videos when they do not last long.

- More and more people are viewing videos on their mobile phones. Short videos open faster when viewed on a mobile phone and so are more likely to gain hits.

- Creating a large quantity of short videos gives you a greater chance of being ranked well on YouTube or Google.

- If you decide to edit the videos, doing so for short videos is easier and simpler than longer duration videos.

- Once on YouTube, short videos usually spread among the community more quickly than long videos.

One of the easiest ways to create videos for local companies is to use a tool like Animoto.com and create a slideshow from pictures of the business. Animoto is very easy to use and allows you to quickly produce high-quality video slideshows of any local business.

Some of my students use a program called Pro Show Gold as an alternative to Animoto because, as Animoto grows in popularity, Social Media Managers need new ways to differentiate their products from the mix. Pro Show Gold provides a comparable service but distinctively presents slideshow videos.

In addition to using Animoto, it's advisable to also take some videos of the company's employees. This is one of the best ways to increase trust and credibility among consumers.

Here is a quick list of some videos you can make for local companies. These are just a few, but the possibilities are endless.

- Quick video presentation of the company and their product
- Where to find the company and their opening hours
- How the products are used
- The main benefits of the products and services
- Testimonials by some customers
- Having customers present the product themselves

Furthermore, try to think about what kinds of videos your company's Facebook fans would like to see. The following is a list of video ideas likely to be well received among Facebook users:

- **Time-lapse videos:** This type of video is taken using extremely slow frame rates over long periods of time. The effect is such that, when played back at normal speeds, events over long durations become more pronounced and observable (i.e. watching a flower bud, or the construction of a new building being completed in 30 seconds). This method is highly recommended for companies in the hospitality sector, like hotels and restaurants, because both of these sectors have very visual products. For example for a restaurant you could create a time-lapse video of a long meal being prepared. You can search for "time-lapse videos" on YouTube and see several examples.

- **Videos explaining your client's Facebook offers:** If your client implements coupons or another form of discount for its Facebook fans, it's important to communicate clearly via video how to redeem these offers and how they work. By connecting a face with the product and services, not just an anonymous text, your client company can strengthen their credibility and trust among its fans.

- **FAQ videos:** Request the Facebook page's fans to ask their biggest questions and then answer them using videos.

- **Customer testimonials:** Video testimonials are a crucial component to effective social media that every company should produce. However, on Facebook, it's equally important that these videos be well edited. One suggestion is to combine clips and make a single compilation of the best testimonials.

- **"Behind the scenes videos":** Videos where you show something that clients don't normally see are well received among Facebook users. For example, a restaurant could show scenes of their chef preparing a specialty plate back in the kitchen - an area typically off-limits to everyday patrons.

You might be thinking that all of this is difficult and requires too much time or technical skill. However, all of these videos can be recorded with a small and easy-to-use camera. How to do so will be explained in the next section.

www.smartsocialmedia.biz/vip

Video Marketing Step 2: Recording

When recording videos, the most important thing is to act quickly! Your first videos are never perfect, but they can be improved over time. By creating a large quantity of videos right away you can outperform any competitors in the local markets.

The first thing to keep in mind when selecting a device is that you do not need a traditional video camera. There are many recording tools today, such as digital cameras that produce the same results at a fraction of the cost. You should, however, use at least one camera that records videos in HD (High Definition) for a more professional end result.

Here are some of my favorite cameras that record good quality video and are also very affordable:

- Sony MHS-TS20 Bloggie Touch Camera - Full 1080p HD video and 12.8-megapixel still pictures. Easy to transfer video to your computer. Small and easy to take with you.

- iPhone 4s - Records high quality HD video Built-in apps let you edit and share video instantly.

For even more professional video recording you can

consider the Canon EOS Rebel T3 12.2 MP digital camera. This can normally be found for under $650 USD on discounted sellers such as Amazon.com. But, just to get started, I would recommend the Sony Bloggie. You can also find quality cameras by Kodak such as the Kodak Playtouch which allows you to insert an external microphone.

I also recommend that you start using your smartphone, such as the iPhone 4s, to create videos. This will save you lots of time and can be done on the go. You will also need to obtain additional camera equipment.

The most important equipment you will need for professional results are a tripod and an external microphone.

- Tripod - you always want to make sure your videos are stable and don't look shaky. When it comes to a tripod, I suggest a Manfrotto, but you can use whichever one you prefer.

- External Microphone - Olympus ME-51S Stereo Microphone.

Tips for filming your videos

- Prepare your client to speak in front of the camera. Many people are very shy and avoid speaking in front of the camera. However, you can coach them and remind them that talking on a video is the same as talking on the phone with a client who wants to get more information about their company. The main thing is that they feel comfortable and relaxed because the viewers will perceive this while watching the video and it can greatly affect the building of trust.

- Choose a good location for filming your video. You could use areas such as beauty spots, picturesque countryside, or the company office where employees may be seen in the background. Never record videos against white walls as the end result will look boring. Having interesting looking backgrounds can make all the difference between the impact of the company's videos versus those of the competition, and also offers an original and unique perspective to the customers.

- For example, businesses in the tourist sector should apply backdrops in the countryside or areas where viewers can appreciate beaches, mountains, valleys, famous monuments, and relevant attractions in the area. This type of backdrop attracts people's attention. Just make sure that the background seen in the filming of the video is related to the overall theme of the video.

- Film videos using natural light. This and the previous point are closely related. It will always be better to take advantage of natural light. Even when filming an interview with an employee or customer inside of a building, the maximum possible levels of natural light should be obtained, such as by positioning the cameras against open windows.

- Focus the frame on the person speaking. The person speaking should be in the middle of the frame. Also, the subject should not be sitting too far back from the camera. Likewise, make sure that viewer can see the eyes of the person speaking as this also helps to build more trust among customers.

Video Marketing Step 3: Promoting

The good news is that there are many great places to promote videos, get consumer views, and marketing exposure for your client.

The first step is to open a YouTube channel for your client, personalize this channel with information about your client, and link it to their company website and Facebook page.

YouTube is the largest video-sharing site. Uploading your videos there will increase the client's chances for ranking highly on first-search results on YouTube and also on the first page of Google search results.

Creating a YouTube channel is completely free. I recommend you begin by uploading at least five videos. When uploading videos, select your keywords carefully and use them in the videos' titles. Try to use keywords related to the geographic location of your client as previously mentioned with the example of an Italian restaurant in Dallas.

On March 2012, YouTube changed its algorithm for ranking videos. Now, in addition to keywords, factors regarding a video's engagement - such as how many people comment or click "like" on it - will also play a role; the more community feedback, the higher the ranking. When doing a series of videos, it's recommended that you encourage people to leave comments or click on the "like" button, or ask people to subscribe to your channel for automatic notification of new content uploads.

In addition to YouTube, you can share your client's videos in many other trafficked places. Here is a list of examples where you can share videos and create more visibility and exposure for your clients:

- **Share the videos on the client's Facebook page** - All of the videos created for your clients should also be added to their Facebook page. Facebook really appreciates video content and it's recommended that you add these videos to Facebook manually. Do not just share the links to where the videos are already uploaded on YouTube. When sharing videos on Facebook, always remember to ask questions and actively engage the page's fans. It's also advisable that you ask the members of the Facebook page about what kinds of video content they would like the company to create and share.

- **Share the videos on other social networks** – If your client has a presence on other social networks like Twitter or Pinterest you can share the videos on these platforms as well.

- **Share the video on your client's website** - Most local businesses lack an engaging and informative website. Posting videos is a great way for them to increase credibility and gain more trust from prospective clients. I recommend putting one video on the main page as a presentation and then creating a section on your client's website where all of the videos can be located - including customer testimonials and video interviews with employees. If your client sells something online (for instance, a hotel with a booking engine on their website), you can create video tutorials on how to make your booking or complete your order. This will also help to increase the trust and confidence from the audience.

Video Marketing Step 4: Creating Your Action Plan

As with Facebook marketing, you should have a generic action plan that can be customized according to the needs of your client.

Planning:

- Send a survey to your client. You can use the same questions as mentioned previously in the section on Facebook. The purpose of this will be to find out whether they have previously done any video marketing and what their main goals for YouTube or video marketing are moving forward. Normally, local companies use videos to boost product sales and increase their credibility and trust among clients.

- If you have done video marketing before, show your client some examples. This will always help them to better understand what video marketing entails and what they can expect from your services.

- Like with Facebook marketing, try to identify the ideal client demographic for whom the videos will be created. Do a quick investigation, searching the main keywords for your client on YouTube and tracking which companies in their sector are already using video marketing.

- Create a list of five video ideas you can make for your clients. As an example, one idea could be to have an employee discussing the company's products and services. Another may be to present customer testimonials. Plan each one such that they all have a specific purpose.

- Create a plan for how you will make these videos, such as using tools like Animoto.com that creates slideshows. I normally recommend asking your client to send you all available photos of their products and then making 2 or 3 such videos with this resource. It's equally important to plan where you will make the client's videos. I suggest doing them on-site at the client's business or facility. Most importantly, always preserve more time to shoot your videos than you think you will need. You never know what might come up.

- Conduct keyword research to find out how your client's customers are searching for products and services on search engines like Google. Google Keyword tool is the most common way to conduct this tracking and it's easy and free to use. Identify 4 or 5 keywords and then mold your videos to fit those terms so that they may be used as titles.

Recording

- Decide which camera you will use to record your videos. Always make sure to record in HD (High Definition).

- Arrange your scenes to have plenty of natural light and, preferably, use an external microphone to make sure the sound is correct. In addition, make sure to use a tripod to steady the filming.

- Help your client to speak in a calm and natural manner. Most people fail to understand that the audience wants to hear normal speech as they would on the phone with a friend. And don't stress about making mistakes as these will only make your video appear more "human".

- Feel free to make some test recordings to check the quality and sound of the recording.

Promoting

- Visit YouTube.com and create a channel for your client by clicking "create account" on the top right hand corner.

- Customize the channel by adding your client's business information such as their location, hours of operation, and links to presence on other social media sites like Facebook.

- Upload the first video on your YouTube channel using the keywords you researched beforehand.

- Add your client's telephone number by using the annotations feature on YouTube.

- Once you have several videos uploaded on the same channel, you can create a playlist of similar topics.

- Share the videos on your client's Facebook page. Also, pose questions along with the posts to engage with the Facebook fans.

- Additionally, you can share the videos on other social networks like Pinterest.

- Analyze the statistics of your videos on YouTube (called "YouTube Analytics"). Check which ones have the most traffic and "likes" and then use this information to create similar videos.

Video Editing - Keeping the Editing To a Minimum

The majority of videos made for local businesses do not require huge amounts of editing or special effects. The most important thing is that, at the end, the company's telephone number and webpage are clearly shown. This can also be accomplished by using YouTube's annotations feature; after uploading your video to YouTube, go to your video link's url and find the button called Annotations (note: you will need to be signed in to your YouTube account to do this).

If you decide to create an intro for the video, do this in a short, simple, and effective way, lasting no longer than 4 or 5 seconds. The purpose of an intro is only for the viewers to get an idea about what they will see later in the video.

Another option for video editing is to use YouTube's program, WeVideo. WeVideo is a cloud-based video editing platform that helps you to conduct simple video editing by editing videos directly in your browser with media files from any device. You can quickly combine clips with music, effects, titles, transitions, and animation. With WeVideo, you can even share videos on social media with one click.

You   can   find   WeVideo   editor   at:

www.youtube.com/create_detail/WeVideo

Some of the more traditional editing programs include iMovie and ScreenFlow for Mac users, and Sony Vegas for PC users. Of these, my favorite program is ScreenFlow because it's much faster than iMovie and also works as a great program to record screen capture tutorial videos.

Going Mobile – Why Smartphones Are a Great Video Marketing Tool

One of the easiest ways of quickly producing video content is by using an iPhone 4 or iPhone 4s, both of which have great video cameras. The advantage of using an iPhone is that, after recording your video, you can easily edit or share it using the phone's apps and you can create videos on to go where ever you are.

The best tripod for the iPhone is the Glif tripod, and can be found at:www.studioneat.com/products/glif-for-iphone-4

As for your iPhone's microphone, you might consider using Boom Mic - easy to insert into any iPhone and which will increase the sound quality of your videos.

http://photojojo.com/store/awesomeness/iphone-boom-mic/

Recommended video applications for the iPhone:

- **iMovie** - Allows you to edit and produce HD videos fast by adding video, photos, music, and sound effects. You can also add professional-looking titles and transitions.

- **Animoto** - Best app for creating amazing looking slideshow videos directly from your iPhone.

- **Splice** - Similar to iMovie but offers extra features like Ken Burns, slow-motion, fast-forward, and custom video trimmer.

- **Vimeo** - Easy-to-use video editor that also allows you to upload your video directly to Vimeo and manage existing videos.

- **Videolicious** - allows you to create great looking videos by quickly turning your video clips and photos into tightly edited masterpieces.

- **Diptic** - allows you to combine multiple photos to create a new image (this is very powerful if you want great looking photos that can be shared on Facebook). These photos can then later be used to create powerful video slideshows.

Common Mistakes with Video Marketing

Some common mistakes made by people just starting as Social Media Managers in creating videos for local companies are listed in the hopes that you can avoid them:

- **Don't buy a traditional camcorder** - Use cameras like Sony Bloggie or others mentioned before. They are small and easy to take with you, and more easily transfer video to your computer than traditional expensive camcorders.

- **Don't hire an actor** - Most of the time, having an actor will only make your video look unnatural and unauthentic. Don't worry if a person says something like, "Ahh, ahh" or other verbal stutters common with poor camera communication – it's not a big deal because these mistakes will make the video more natural and transparent. Small mistakes like these will make the video perfect for local companies who want to highlight the fact that they are there to serve the community. They are not professional video creators.

- **Don't spend too much time editing videos -** Keep your videos short and simple. If you need to shoot the video several times, do it. Many takes is normally better than spending hours editing the video. Previously, I mentioned it's best to use the editing features inside YouTube. For example, YouTube annotations and YouTube's new WeVideo editor can be used to add the url or phone number directly into the videos.

- **Don't overcomplicate things** - Some clients I have helped were stuck believing that video marketing is a hard and complicated process taking up a great deal of time. However, due to modern technology and the wide variety of tools now available, good-quality material can be produced fairly quickly. And remember, the main focus is on creating a large quantity of short videos.

Video Marketing Case Study – Mario Schumacher

Mario Schumacher of Costa Blanca, Spain, is a Social Media Manager of the tourism portal ILoveCostaBlanca.com. Mario is known well within the industry for creating effective video marketing. One such implementation is his use of video interviews with people involved behind-the-scenes in the portal IloveCostaBlanca.com. Additionally, Mario has video marketing experience with political campaigns, having helped a candidate to win the election with the aid of Facebook and video marketing.

"In the political campaign, what really worked for us was creating very personal videos where the candidate answered questions sent by everyday citizens on Facebook. With these videos, we wanted to convey the human side of the candidates and avoid shooting productions that would come across as too professional, creating a disconnect with the people. Additionally, what worked very well for us was preparing a series of 40 difficult questions that citizens could ask the candidate before the campaign started. Planning the content in advance this way helped create a powerful campaign presence in social media and I highly recommend these tips to any Social Media Manager with a politician as a client. Also, I encourage lots of video interviews as a quick way to generate quality content on YouTube and advance a dominant ranking in Google searches."

You   can   find   the   YouTube   channel   for
ILoveCostaBlanca.com   at
www.youtube.com/ilovecostablanca

Outsource and Grow Your Business

Once you have few a clients, it's highly recommendable to start outsourcing and delegating part of your work so that you can leverage your time and resources. This is the only way to have fast and scalable growth for your business without losing your mind or becoming completely frustrated. You need to find what you like to do the most and outsource the rest. Some people choose to focus on Facebook marketing and then outsource video marketing, for example.

Some successful Social Media Managers focus on customer retention and leave most of the fulfillment work to their team. Since they have created a linear business system allowing them to leverage their time, they can spend time improving the marketing of their services.

Some key areas you can outsource include:

- Graphic design: For example, creation of the Facebook landing page image, or YouTube and Twitter background.

- Video creation: Creation of the Animoto videos.

- YouTube channel creation and video optimization.

- Article writing and proofreading.

- Creating cover image for Facebook page.

- Facebook page management and updating.

In order to build a big and lasting business, you should start considering outsourcing some of your social media tasks. There are several sites where you can find talented freelance workers who are willing to complete different types of tasks. Some of the most commonly used sites are: elance.com, craigslist.org, rendacoder.com, vworker.com, and fiverr.com

Before you begin outsourcing, remember to establish a clear plan for your goals over the next 3 to 6 months. Determine what tasks specifically you would like to outsource. This will help you to achieve clarity and, later on, it will be easier to manage your business.

Always be sure to maintain an open line of communication with your team members; convey with clarity what is needed and by when. One useful tool for communicating with your team members is Skype, for live video conferencing. You may also be interested in using Jing (www.jingproject.com) project, which allows you to create quick tutorials that can be shared with your team members.

Increasing Your Income through Course Offerings

Once you begin offering social media management to local businesses, it's quite possible that you will find yourself being asked to train company personnel in effectively managing Facebook and video marketing for themselves. You can do this even without experience by following some simple guidelines.

Furthermore, most companies are not looking for the most well-established keynote speaker on the topic of Facebook or video marketing, but simply want to listen to someone who knows more than they do on the subject and who can tell them about the benefits of its use. Providing customized social media courses to companies can be really refreshing when combined with your typical Facebook and YouTube account management, and it's not nearly as difficult as some might think.

Personally, I enjoy providing these trainings on social media because they give me the chance to personally consult and help that particular company. I recommend offering either half or full day trainings and giving your clients the opportunity to later purchase additional consulting hours if they have specific questions or needs.

The following is a list of key insights that have proved helpful to me over the years and that will help you when just beginning in the field:

- Always send a detailed survey to the company beforehand about their products, current level of knowledge in social media, and any specific challenges with which they need your help.

- Be clear on any client expectations with the training. For instance, one client might need ideas on how to use video marketing to create more awareness of their product, or how to improve video ranking on YouTube and Google. They might not be interested in Facebook at that point, and it wouldn't do either of you any good to spend time working in undesired areas. Do your homework and prepare to fit your client's needs.

- Always be on time and begin the session by letting the client's employees introduce themselves.

- Try to ask questions of the employees during a training session. Keep the atmosphere open and interactive so that the participants don't feel you are just giving a lecture.

- Before concluding, summarize your presentation by highlighting the key action items the client needs to implement.

- After the training, perhaps within a week, send another survey to your clients to receive feedback on what they felt to be most valuable and on how you might improve next time.

One of the key benefits to giving social media training for companies is that it will increase your reputation as a consultant. Companies will start to view you as an expert who provides personalized, valuable training rather than just another salesman offering social media promotions.

www.smartsocialmedia.biz/vip

Additional Online Marketing Services

As a Social Media Manager, I encourage you to start with Facebook and video marketing and build a very good relationship with your client. This will allow you later on to offer additional services to improve the client's online presence. However, don't start offering additional services without the proper training on how companies should use them.

The following is a list of some additional services you can offer to your clients:

- **Create a Google+ page** – Google+ pages (not to be confused with Google+ Local places), similar to Facebook, offers many features for companies by allowing them to share important information. Google+ does not yet have the same kind of huge user-base as Facebook, but the service is rapidly growing. It offers interesting benefits to companies that should be explored as well. One of its best aspects is that Google Plus will be integrated with all of Google's other services and, therefore, will end up being a very important social network. Likewise, a presence on Google Plus normally helps the company on their Google search engine listings.
  Url: www.google.com/+/business

- **Creating and managing a company page on Linkedin** Linkedin is the largest online social network focused exclusively on business people. It offers great possibilities for networking and building relationships among the key people in your industry. Linkedin is especially useful for companies that work in a business-to-business environment. Url: www.linkedin.com

- **Build and manage Twitter accounts** - Twitter has been one of the most popular social media sites for a long time, however, most businesses will find Facebook and YouTube much more valuable. Twitter works great for journalists, media personalities, celebrities, and big brands with a huge customer base. Small businesses can use it, but I recommend first focusing on Facebook and YouTube. It works great as place to conduct customer support, send interesting notifications, and interact with prospective customers. Url: www.twitter.com

- **Deliver reputation management services** - More and more consumers search a company's name and their product on Google before making a buying decision. Due to this, there exists a great opportunity to help companies monitor their online reputation and make improvements. This is a more complex service and I don´t recommend starting it without the proper information and training.

- **Create a presence on Google+ Local Places** – Google+ Local (previously "Google Places") offers an excellent way for local companies to create a listing and optimize their presence on Google's local search results. Google+ local pages include basic information about businesses including a phone number, hours of operation, a map of the business's physical location, and also reviews and ratings. In the long run, it's also recommended that you get patrons of your client's company to leave reviews on the Google+ local listing.

- **Start to use Pinterest** - Pinterest is one of fastest growing social networking sites around and serves as a great platform to share and comment on photos. Before starting with Pinterest, make sure your client has a strong presence on both Facebook and YouTube. Then consider whether Pinterest is a proper additional platform for your client. For example, local businesses with numerous visual products will have more to benefit - such as a local flower store, cupcake bakery, or restaurant. Sharing photos on a site like this will allow them to circulate visually appetizing advertisements of their products. By contrast, businesses focusing on non-visual services may not have as much to gain by sharing pictures. The most effective way to use Pinterest is to avoid the temptation of self-promotion; simply share your beautiful photos and comment on other users'. In general, be active inside this Social Network. Pinterest also has a very well made iPhone application, which can help you to

use this source on the go. Url:
www.pinterest.com

- **Start to use Instagram** - Instagram is a unique photo sharing application that works on the iPhone and Android platforms, and which Facebook recently acquired for one billion USD. As with Pinterest, Instagram is most suitable for local businesses with visual products of which you can take and share plenty of photos. Many big brands like Starbucks and Ben & Jerry's are leveraging the power of Instagram well, allowing them to share unique and exciting pictures directly with consumers. Since Facebook has bought Instagram, it has become important to have a presence on their site, and I consider it to be more prominent of a photo-sharing site than Pinterest. However, as always, remember to consider the amount of time both sites can take away from you to manage and only use them with companies with an abundance of photos to share.

- **Mobile marketing services** - Mobile marketing is becoming huge as more and more consumers use their smartphones to buy things online. There are many opportunities here because companies will need mobile versions of their website. Leverage the correct use of QR codes, learn how to use Smartphones effectively for business, and even create mobile applications.

- **Create a "check-in" special on Foursquare** – Foursquare is a location-based social network for smartphones. This service offers companies a great opportunity to promote their presence by creating special discounts for customers who "check-in" at their venue using the mobile Foursquare application. It's recommended to post stickers inside the premises of the business that include the foursquare logo and inform visitors about the special. Restaurants, for example, could offer a free dessert for customers who purchase an entrée and "check-in" on foursquare. Foursquare is especially relevant for restaurants, coffee shops, and local stores in urban areas. Additionally, this service allows business owners to get to know and better connect with their customers.

- **Submitting a website to local business directories** – As local marketing gets bigger and bigger, powerful directories and sites where local companies can add their listings are being developed. Here are some of the best local business directories:
  - www.thumbtack.com
  - www.servicemagic.com
  - www.yelp.com
  - www.local.com
  - www.citysearch.com
  - www.insiderpages.com
  - www.kudzu.com
  - www.shopcity.com

As you can see, there are numerous opportunities for delivering value to your clients. These are just some of the options. Many of my coaching clients only deliver one or two services, typically Facebook and/or YouTube. Focus is extremely crucial for your long-term success, so try to avoid getting distracted. Only offer services when you have received the proper training on how to deliver them.

Getting Your First Clients

Some people just beginning their career as a Social Media Manager think that delivering Facebook and YouTube marketing services are the only important skills for the job. However, the most crucial skill is attracting the right clients for your business. In the long run, two of the cornerstone elements for the profession are one's personal branding and reputation as a local marketing consultant. However, when you start, it's vitally important to understand the key dynamics of attracting the right kind of clients for your work.

The following results are taken from a survey conducted among my Smart Social Media Freedom System students and will give you an indication of how to find more clients when working as a Social Media Manager.

Question 1: How did you get your customers: through friends, by visiting them in their own businesses, the Internet, newspaper ads, or by applying other techniques?

Summary of the answers:

• Visiting the prospective client's business directly: 28.6%

• Recommendation of friends or family: 25.7%

• Contacting via social networks, e.g. Facebook: 14.3%

- Contacting via email: 11.5%

- Customers were previously clients of my other services: 5.7%

- Referrals by other customers: 5.7%

- I am a customer of theirs and now offered my services: 5.7%

- Offering a one-month free trial period: 2.8%

These results suggest that the most successful method for finding new clients is by visiting them in person or by recommendation through friends and family members. Also, contacting companies via Facebook seems to be a successful method. Many Social Media Manager build their own Facebook page and openly share techniques and tips. This outreach attracts a lot of companies who might later be interested in your services.

In summation, much of the clientele building as a Social Media Manager comes from pre-existing relationships, either directly with the client or by association through referral. This network building aspect to being successful in the field is an extremely important lesson to be learned out of the gate. I strongly recommend that you ponder how to use these various methods for building your clientele base.

For some, the first client is normally done free of charge and used as a way for obtaining testimonial and referrals. However, the number of free clients should always be limited because it's important that both you and your clients value the service you provide.

Question 2: What techniques or strategies do you use to close the deal with your clients?

• I show the many benefits and usage statistics of social media: 25.7%

• I provide examples of successful companies who are already using social media: 20.0%

• I offer several service plans at various prices: 17.2%

• I offer additional services at no extra cost: 14.3%

• I show them the benefits of a Facebook page with statistics: 11.4%

• I offer a one-month trial with free advice: 8.5%

• I offer a trial period of my services: 8.5%

• I offer a mutual exchange of services: 5.7%

• I explain the long and short-term goals: 2.8%

• I offer a free web analysis: 2.8%

These results indicate that showing usage statistics of social media along with examples of other companies who have already successfully implement social media really helps small businesses to understand the benefits of hiring someone to run their Facebook page or YouTube channel.

Additional successful strategies include: offering varied plans with different prices, offering to do some additional service(s) with no extra cost, and offering some kind of trial period (however you might structure that arrangement).

Remember, the value you bring to the marketplace will begin to determine your service rates, so create a reputation of treating your clients extremely well and always going overboard when it comes to the delivery of services. This will help you to get more referrals than you need and really take your business to the next level.

Additional ideas of getting your first customers

The following are some ideas on how to land your first client. I find this to be a crucial step for everyone who is just starting out as a Social Media Manager. You will then also feel much more confident later when implementing Facebook or video marketing.

I should remind my readers that, before starting to work with your client, you should have the proper education on how to deliver Facebook and YouTube Marketing.

- **Offer free services** - The fastest way to gain the trust of potential clients is by offering some services for free. By providing a sample of your work, you can showcase your abilities and entice them into contracting for greater services.

  Some suitable free services you can provide include:

  Website analysis: consider sites like www.seorush.com and others that create complete analysis of any website

  Create a short market analysis: simply search the main keywords related to the activity of the business on Google, YouTube, and Facebook, and create a word document with your findings illustrating which companies are in the top positions on these sites. Personally, I also like using www.socialmention.com to analyze what's being said about the company or their product.

Create a quick video and upload it to YouTube: services like Animoto.com let you create a slideshow video simply by uploading photos and using their ready-made video templates. These are just some of the ideas of different services you can provide for companies in order to show them your value as a Social Media Manager, and ways to start a conversation on how you can better help them with their social media efforts.

- **Contact companies who already spend money on advertising** - Another proven method for finding new clients is to go after companies who are already spending money on advertising. You can search the Yellow Pages to see which companies have the biggest ads there. Also, you can go on Google and type some generic search terms that include your location and the sector, for example "plumber in Miami." Then, identify businesses who advertise on Google Adwords; those listings normally appear on the right-hand side of the Google results page.

  Remember that these companies don't know you, which normally equates to not trusting you and, therefore, you need to provide value to them before starting to work with them.

- **Focus on companies that are new in your area**, they normally don't have established clientele and are open to finding out how to use the power of Facebook or videos to launch their operations.

- **Focus on companies that are family owned** and stay away from franchises or chains such as with hotels or restaurants. Family owned or privately owned companies can quickly make decisions and are normally easier to work with than larger companies where the decision-making takes longer.

- **Be patient and listen to your possible clients and their needs.** Ask questions such as, "What is your marketing plan?" Or, more specifically, "What is your marketing plan with social media?" These are very powerful questions and I learned them from a marketing legend, David Preston. You will find that simply listening to your possible clients and asking them powerful questions will open many doors.

- **Offer a referral fee to anyone who refers new clients to you**. You can offer 15% - 30% of your first month's fee to a person who refers to you any new clients. This is a great way of expanding your business since it will give you new clients for free. In addition, always ask your current clients if they know any business owners who would need help with social media in order to get more referrals.

- **Create a powerful metaphor to describe the value of your services.** One of my most successful students, Annabel Lleonart, compares a company's social media presence to the traffic of a city. She asks her clients, "Would you rather have your store on Madison Avenue in

Manhattan or in some distant industrial area in the outskirts of town?" Here, "Madison Avenue" represents a well-optimized Facebook page because Facebook is where most people spend their days. In contrast, not having a presence on social media is like establishing your store in the wastelands where nobody will ever come to shop.

These kinds of examples help your clients to see the value of your services and the benefits of using social media by relating your work to something everyone can understand.

- **Use postcard marketing to solicit companies and present their services**. Today, when everyone receives too much email, this alternative provides a more personal touch in approaching gold contacts (local companies). Also, this way you can personalize images or graphics specific to the target company - for example, a search engine screenshot showing a diminished rank among search results on YouTube. The best service for this kind of marketing is "Send Out Cards" which you can find online at www.sendoutcards.com/141411

- **Consider avoiding the title "Social Media Manager" when you first introduce yourself to companies.** I know this might sound contradictory, however, according to the experience of many of my successful students, small business owners get frustrated and confused when hearing new terms like "Social Media Manager" or "Community Manager". Those titles may be very well known among big brands, but for others I recommend you present yourself as an "social media consultant", "small business consultant" or "local marketing consultant" that trains and consults companies on how to better leverage social media and Internet Marketing.

The title of "consultant" is widely known and business owners of all sizes and can associate it with someone who helps companies to grow and prosper through specialized expertise and knowledge.

Recommendations for New Social Media Managers

In this book, you will find valuable tips from current social media managers and industry experts. I also share a bit of my own back-story about the challenges and victories I faced when just getting started.

Consulting and helping local clients with social media gives me great pleasure and honor. This line of work offers opportunities to provide companies with real value and to help them improve their marketing. One of the main challenges I faced when starting out was managing my time, often spending countless late-night hours in front of a computer creating videos or improving my client's presence on Facebook.

Fortunately, I learned to outsource and delegate part of the workload. I highly recommend you consider doing the same from the very start because it will free up some of your time that can be better used obtaining new clients and working on more complicated tasks. These days, there are numerous sites for outsourcing such work that did not exist when I began. That being said, my main recommendation is that you start delegating part of your work as soon as possible.

In the next section, I will share further insights to help you achieve success in this field and to optimize your work as a Social Media Manager.

Tips related to working with clients

- Make and execute a plan laying out the logistics for your company. Indicate how many clients you should have in the first 6 months, how much you will charge each one, and how much of your time you will dedicate.

- Once you obtain larger clients, it's fundamental that you have a written agreement with them and clearly identify when the project is set to begin, when it is projected to ends, and any other relevant details to the contract.

- Always show interest and curiosity in your client's products and business. In general, the better you know what they offer, the more interesting and valuable your work will become. Plus, it will be easier for you to sell them additional services.

- Value communication with your client. Try to respond quickly to their emails and always maintain an open dialogue. This will show your client that you care about them and their business.

- Value your client's opinions and points of view. For example, if your client does not believe in video or YouTube marketing but is excited about Facebook marketing, focus on the latter. You can always provide educational material on alternative media possibilities to help your client understand the many additional benefits, but be patient and respectful of their opinion.

Tips related to your personal growth

- **Develop your personal leadership skills** - Many people just starting out as a Social Media Manager will find it to be a totally different working environment than what they are used to with the typical 9 to 5 office job. Everyone agrees that you need to be able to get out of your comfort zone, take action even when you are afraid to do so, and learn to work within a constantly changing environment. However, all this is well worth it; you can achieve a freedom otherwise unthinkable in the typical office job.

  Developing leadership skills will help you get through difficult times, become more disciplined, and to move forward and enjoy your work more. I study personal development or leadership by reading and listening to materials from some of my favorite authors, such as: Wayne Dyer, T Harv Eker, John Maxwell, Jay Abraham, Anthony Robbins and others. I'm very grateful for the inspiration and knowledge gained from these masters. Try to find people that you can most connect with and enjoy, and set aside time on your calendar for personal growth.

- **Exercise frequently** - Today, there are many people who work online as freelancers from home or an office and spend most of their time in front of their computer. This leaves out necessary physical activity - exercise of the body. Personally, I try to do physical exercise like going to gym or jogging every day for at least 30 minutes. I've found this to be the fastest way to increase my productivity, keep my mind clear, and help me to concentrate better. Doing daily exercise is the fastest way to increase your energy level and increase your productivity. This in turn will increase your earnings.

- **Be comfortable with new trends and a constantly changing working environment** - Internet technologies and social media are continuously changing and, as a Social Media Manager, you should not be too worried about it. Remember that your primary focus is on providing value to your clients and helping them communicate better with their customers online. When new trends or social media sites pop up, ask yourself, "Will being on this site bring value to my client?"

A prime example of the typical changes you can expect within this industry are the many new novelties Facebook introduces on a revolving basis. More or less, every 12 months, Facebook tends to introduce some big change. Most people normally strongly dislike the changes introduced, but recognizing that adjustments are normal in this industry, I always look at the Facebook model with an open mind, willing to learn how my clients can benefit from these alterations. I recommend you do the same.

- **Constantly develop your personal branding** - There have never before been as many opportunities available to improve and grow your personal branding as there are today. All of us have the ability to create videos, write articles, upload photos, and share part of our day-to-day work using social media. You should also be aware that many small business owners will search for your online presence (i.e. Google your name) before hiring you. It's fairly simple to rank the first page of Google with your own name if you use it on the title of the content you share online (including videos, photos, and articles).

Some of my students have found it useful to share tips and insights from their work with clients on their personal website or Facebook page. These insights could sound something like, "Yesterday, when working with a client of mine who operates a restaurant, I discovered…." Sharing snippets like this from your work does not take long but can be extremely powerful. Also, consider sharing quick video tips on what you have learned in your work as a Social Media Manager in a video format; create videos where you present what type of services you normally provide and how you work with your customers. Improving your personal brand will help differentiate yourself from your competition and build credibility with your potential clients.

www.smartsocialmedia.biz/vip

Recommended Tools and Resources

Here is a list of tools you might find useful as a Social Media Manager:

Social media management

- HootSuite – One of the leading tools for monitoring and managing all of your social networking accounts in a single forum. HootSuite allows you to pre-schedule messages thereby improving productivity. Currently, integration is offered with: Facebook, LinkedIn, Twitter, Google+ Pages, FourSquare, MySpace, and Wordpress. HootSuite also allows you to track certain keywords, like "restaurant New York," so that you can immediately see where people are discussing keywords related to your client's company. Url: www.hootsuite.com

- Sprout Social – Offers similar features to HootSuite, including scheduling updates and monitoring conversations. However, Sprout Social applies a more visually attractive dashboard, providing you with an overall view of what is happening on your social media accounts.

You can also obtain comprehensive reports and analytics - very useful information you can relay to your clients. Additionally, you can assign tasks to your team members or use the iPhone application on the go. Url: www.sproutsocial.com

Client and contact management

- Docs.google.com - Google's free set of tools which allows users to share documents and conduct collaborative work with others. This is ideal for sharing Excel spreadsheets with your clients.

- Highrisehq.com - Very popular customer relationship management tool allowing users to keep a list of prospective client and manage contacts.

Photo editing

- picmonkey.com - free online image editor tool, useful for cropping and resizing images.

- http://pixlr.com/editor - another very useful image e editor with some similar functions to Photoshop.

Communications with clients

- Skype.com - most commonly used instant messaging and video conferencing system. Skype video calls are recommended when you need to conduct virtual client meetings as seeing each other can help to increase trust and confidence.

- Jingproject.com - free and effective program that allows you to share screenshots or short videos of up to 5 minutes easily with your team members or clients.

- Meetingburner.com - Professional webinar service provider allowing users a free conference room for up to 50 people.

- Gotomeeting.com - the leading webinar software, offering high quality webinar facilities and the ability to record HD video conferences.

Sending and sharing files

- Dropbox.com - the leading online sharing program that works great for sharing important documents with your customers or sending large files.

- Yousendit.com - another application for sharing important files and archives with team members and clients.

Market research

- Social Bakers – Offers free statistics for social networks such as Facebook, YouTube, Twitter, LinkedIn, and Google Plus. For example, you can see a comparison of major US brands on Facebook or how many users reside in the United States. For a small charge, a Social Bakers Pro account allows you to monitor your Facebook pages, as well as offering illustrations for various statistics such as the engagement rate (the number of interactions to a post - comments and likes - divided by the number of fans). Url: www.socialbakers.com

- Google Keyword Tool – Great free tool which allows you to find and track competing websites using main keywords that your client's customers are searching. These keywords are very useful to incorporate in YouTube videos and blog articles to optimize their ranking.
  Url:adwords.google.com/select/KeywordToolExt ernal

- Google Insights – Excellent tool to discover search volume patterns related to different keywords and geographical areas where certain keywords are being searched the most. This kind of information is very useful and should be included in the reports you send to your clients.
  Url: www.google.com/insights/search

- Google Alerts – Commonly used tool that sends you email updates of new content uploaded onto the Internet based upon certain keywords tracked. It's recommended that you follow multiple keywords including the name of your client, their competitor's name, etc.
  Url: www.google.com/alerts

Case Study Interviews

The following section includes powerful interviews with people just like you who started from nothing and are now successful Social Media Managers and local business consultants. These stories serve to provide inspiration and insight into how others got started, what their difficulties were, and how they obtained clients.

Fabian Herrera - Argentina

Please provide your profession prior to becoming a Social Media Manager.

I live in Argentina in a town called Rafaela. I am an architect by profession, but have always been very interested in jobs dealing with the Internet and social media. I have found the field to be very interesting and I have grown more passionate about it than architecture. The job market and expectations for social media is constantly growing.

Please share some of the strategies and techniques that have helped you to attract customers.

When I was starting out, almost by an accident, I ran into an old friend who asked me, "What are you doing these days?" I told him, "I'm an Internet consultant," and he asked, "What is that exactly? I would like to know because I might need your help" I told him that I specialize in helping companies gain a better presence on

Facebook. He got excited and asked, "Could you check out my Facebook presence and advise on how I could improve?" And, that's how I got started. As he is my friend, I decided to give him the first month for free in exchange for him later referring me 4 contacts.

Looking back, this was a great strategy and I recommend everyone to do the same. Although you are doing it free, getting a testimonial from one business is worth a lot in the long run. Get yourself into action and you will get a sense of how long delivering all of this work will take you, so that later you may better scale your business. What works for me is to tell friends and contacts that "I'm an internet consultant," or that "I'm an online marketing consultant," or that "I help companies on Facebook." This is much clearer than saying, "I'm a Social Media Manager" - something they probably don't understand and which might confuse them. Using these strategies, it's not difficult to generate new clients simply by talking with some old colleagues or friends I know.

Tell us what services and prices you have set for each of the services you perform. Is it a flat rate or a custom rate for each customer?

Currently, I offer marketing planning for small businesses, specializing in marketing on Facebook including personalized Facebook Landing Pages. Many clients ask me to prepare for them a new website and the price will depend on the company. But, normally, it's approximately US$600 to US$1000.

I also charge US$150 per month for managing Facebook and Twitter, as well as for creating a Facebook landing page. This also includes weekly statistics and information I send to the client.

I don't actually create content for my clients - I teach them to create it for themselves. Also, I do content planning sessions with them and advise them on how to publish quality content on Facebook.

How many clients do you have in total, and how did you get them? What methods did you use?

Currently, I have 16 clients. I found them by using different crossing strategies, such as networking through colleagues, phone contacts, and various other "soft" strategies such as Twitter, Facebook, and small advertising campaigns including Facebook Ads. I have had great results with this plan and highly recommend advertising in Facebook, directing people to your Facebook page where you may present your services to a wide audience. Also, Twitter has helped me find clients from different countries and industries.

Do you do the job yourself or do you outsource or delegate work to other people?

Outsourcing and organizing my work has been the biggest challenge for me. I highly recommend that everyone start to do so from the beginning to grow faster. Right now, I'm hiring one person to do the Facebook pages for me and I just supervise. Also, my daughter is interested to start working with me and soon she will begin helping me with administrative issues.

As to the content itself, like Facebook updates, I don't do it myself but I teach my clients on how they do it look over that they do it the right way.

How has your life changed since you became Social Media Manager?

I see big possibilities and, thanks to my activity on Facebook, some companies have asked me to run social media seminars here in Argentina. I see big opportunities everywhere.

Right now, I'm also very busy organizing my job. Once my daughter begins working with me I will have more free time and I'm really looking forward for it. But, in general, I'm very excited about the sector and all of the possibilities.

What are some specific strategies that have helped your business grow?

Facebook advertising has been the biggest factor. Facebook is the best option when you offer something special like free landing pages; this is something business owners like a lot. At the moment, I'm mostly just working with my current clients and not doing much advertising. Later on, when I need more clients, I will use Facebook advertising by generating very targeted ads only for small business owners.

The other thing is to have email and text ready to send your clients, as well as Skype. It's important to respond quickly to customer inquiries - something that they will appreciate and later make it easier to close the sale.

I normally try to get the meeting as soon as possible. Speed is also important in sending out proposals very quickly.

What would you say are some of the key qualities to be a successful Social Media Manager?

You need to enjoy being in contact with people; because that is one of the skills you will most need. You need to like people and enjoy helping them.

- Learn the basic steps and take action all of the time.
- Be humble; ask for help and consult with the right mentor.
- Move forward quickly while always maintaining your best quality (when you send proposals, communicate with clients, etc.)
- Learn from your mentor and apply what you learn

Annabel Lleonart, Social Media Manager, Barcelona, Spain

Please provide your profession prior to becoming a Social Media Manager.

For 11 years, I was the Director of Restoration for 2 restaurants located in the Hotel Granollers, a city hotel in the Barcelona province. Currently, I still work on restoration and divide my time, devoting a minimum of 5 hours daily to my work as Social Media Manager.

Please share some of the strategies and techniques that have helped you to attract customers.

My current strategy is to advertise by "word of mouth" through friends and acquaintances. I tell them about my company, The Social Media Team, and its services and they then find companies looking for this Social Media Manager service. When people ask me what I do, I tell them that I help companies find their place in social networks, overcome their fears, and accomplish their goals. Today we are servicing 9 companies across a wide array of industries, including an agency, a copy shop, a hotel, 2 restaurants, a couple of hostels, a security company, an industrial machinery company, a gas station, and a company specializing in horses.

Tell us what services and prices you have set for each of the services you perform. Is it a flat rate or a custom rate for each customer?

Our services are extensive. We provide training to businesses, create and set targets in different social networks (such as Facebook, YouTube, LinkedIn, Google +, or Twitter), and also can manage a company's entire social network, continuously creating and improving content, and developing reports and reviews. Our prices are customized to the customer's needs. This can range from 150€ to 800€ per month, depending on the hours needed for each company. So far, customers have seemingly been most interested in Facebook and I always mention it when we speak.

a) What do you tell the customers so they can understand that they need to include their company in the social networks? b) How do you start business with the customers (showing a video, providing a dossier..?)

I try to explain that social networks are another means of communication that can't be ignored, even if they dislike or are afraid of them. This is where both their current and potential customers are, as well as their competitors, and it is where they can demonstrate a transparency and willingness to communicate. Before my first visit, I make a very detailed study of the company's presence on the Internet arena, analyzing their website, if they are present in any social networks, and how they work that out. I study the tendencies of their sector and, with all this information, I am able to give a better (targeted) sales pitch. I usually take between 1 to 2 hours and generate a 3-page report for the client, depending on how active the company is on social networks. When the company realizes I'm well informed and took my time to do my job; trust is built and they grow more receptive and open to explaining their needs.

Do you do the job yourself, or do you outsource or delegate work to other people?

At the moment, I do the work with the help of my two partners who are engaged in design and sales.

How has your life changed since you became Social Media Manager?

This work has taken most of my free time, but it is so satisfactory that I wouldn't change it for anything. It makes me feel like I'm always up-to-date and am always finding something new to learn.

What are some specific strategies that have helped your business grow?

That would be a complete adaptation to customers and their needs; knowing what they want, thinking that they might need more. It is a world that many customers don't like but know they should be there, so it is important to slowly show them that they have made a good decision. As an example of this "adaptation," one of our customers is in the hosteling business and competence is very active on Facebook. When I gave them my proposal, I suggested for them to be as active as the competition but with more valuable content, which they considered to be excessive. So instead, we started slowly, with a few posts per month instead of per week, so that they could begin to feel comfortable and capable of creating daily content.

What would you say are some of the key qualities to be a successful Social Media Manager?

Having lots of common sense, great empathy, and listening. Also, organizing and automatizing everyday tasks, because we touch many keys and vast sectors.

In your opinion, is there any aspect that you think is more important to highlight in the work of a Social Media Manager?

Knowing very well what people expect from you and clearly defining your services to the company, thus avoiding confusion that can generate a lot of extra work and create an unsatisfied customer.

Luz Velásquez,Social Media Manager, Los Angeles, USA

What was your occupation before becoming a Social Media Manager?

Before becoming a Social Media Manager, I worked with my husband in our own business and devoted the rest of my time to learning about the benefits of the Internet, especially the social networks for businesses. However, I felt very frustrated in that I couldn't implement what I was learning. That is, not until December 2011 when I was able to achieve something through my efforts and Lasse's program – Smart Social Media Freedom System.

For me, the program has been very helpful and has shortened my learning curve. The way in which Lasse teaches social media management skills with his program's videos has shortened the time it would have taken me to learn it by myself.

When I started the program, it took me a week to study all the videos and apply what I learned. To my surprise, that same week I started working with a customer for whom I managed a campaign on both Facebook and YouTube.

As a Social Media Manager, what services are you currently offering?

I offer the following services: Facebook page (timeline) creation; business strategy formulation as well as Facebook and YouTube monitoring, such as replying to messages, posting articles, sharing pictures, interacting with groups related to the market niche to find followers; and managing the advertising campaign on Facebook.

Also, on YouTube: creating videos and search keywords to achieve a higher ranking for my customers' videos.

How many customers do you have in total and what methods have you used to obtain them?

I currently have 5 clients. All of them are local businesses in the area where I live, for now. I have found that the best strategy is in sharing FREE information on the benefits offered by social media. I focus on creating the relationship, not getting into discussions. I just simply show the many benefits my work can bring and let that do all of the convincing.

Lasse also provides a survey in the Social Media Manager program, which I have presented to the last two companies I have worked with. I've found that it helped by improving my professionalism and has become a critical part of the search for new local customers.

My clients are from a wide range of varying sectors, including Mental Health, Insurance Agency, Court Interpreter, Natural Products Shop, Sales and Safety Service for Homes and Businesses (keys, safes, etc.), and so forth.

When I speak with a customer for the first time, I always begin by asking, "How is your company's presence on social networks?" Depending on their response, I will either offer my services or share some information that will raise their curiosity in what social networks can offer to improve their brand.

Please mention some strategies and techniques that help you to attract and get more customers

- Creating a relationship: The way I do this is by asking them what they think about Facebook and YouTube in publicizing their business and, according to their answer, will either continue talking with them or simply hand them my business card and say, "I am Social Media Manager, I help entrepreneurs like yourself to create, develop, and execute social media campaigns. That is, I make more people aware of your product or service through Facebook and YouTube. If you're interested in getting more customers and differentiating yourself from the competition, I'm here to help."

- Sharing free information related to social networks: For me, this is the key. There is a lot of misinformation floating around about the use and benefits of social networks for entrepreneurs. What I write in my blog about social networks and the number of users they have is very surprising to new customers. I explain what social networks are for, the difference between a user profile and a business profile on Facebook.

- Listening to the customer and respecting their opinion: When a customer talks, I listen and show respect. It's important to say things like "That's right, but what if..." I don't argue with anyone.

- Mastery of the subject and expressing myself fluently: It's important to speak their language and make sure that they truly understand what you're saying. If they can't understand you, they can't learn what you have to offer.

- Lots of patience

Tell us about the services and pricing you have set. Is it a flat fee or a customized fee for each customer?

The fee depends on what each customer needs. However, I look for clients who are used to paying for advertising in other print media because they understand the benefits of advertising.

Fees start at $500, and range up to $1200 or $ 1500. The higher end includes monitoring their blog, answering comments, updates, etc.

Do you do the work yourself, or do you outsource or delegate the work to others?

At first, I did most of the work. But time is money, so now I delegate work such as: graphic design, blog creation... etc. Since the main idea is to grow, I'm looking to create partnerships with other Social Media Managers.

How has your life changed since you became a Social Media Manager?

Actually, my life changed completely, a 180-degree turn. I got out of a very stormy relationship without a dollar to my name or knowing what to do. Now, thanks to the social media program that I learned with Lasse, I have a profession with a great future that I can perform with pride and passion. I'm very sure of myself and have knowledge in a field crucially important to any competitive business. As with medicine, where health is a human need and you need an expert to get better, or the law, where a legal professional is needed to help you solve a particular problem, Social Media Managers are trained to help businessmen solve issues of competition and marketability by promoting their businesses and advising them on how to get more customers. In short, we get the customers and help businesses achieve successful results.

I believe working as a Social Media Manager is a profession with a future. It is the opportunity to create a social change in the mindset of businessmen, helping them adapt to a changing world where the social arena is one of the most influential factors for people in buying products and services. A Social Media Manager is now a fundamental part for growth in any business sector because the social influence he/she can achieve will determine that company's success.

What are some specific strategies that have helped your business grow?

Adding value to businessmen by offering free information; maintaining an attitude that tells businessmen I'm interested in helping them, not just earning their money; also, speaking with confidence.

Also, I use a little-known saying, "join your worst enemy". Whether you like it or not, your business needs to be in social networks because people will see what you offer, what your current customers say about you, and so on.

What would you say are some of the essential qualities for becoming a successful Social Media Manager?

- Being disciplined
- Bringing order to the work
- Having schedules
- Being responsible, doing your job
- Making sure to be constantly learning and growing as a person to help you overcome your fears.
- Being tolerant of the customer, not forcing or imposing your criteria. Focusing on the benefits for your customer which means making every effort to achieve the goals stated with the customer first and then obtaining your reward.

You must look after your reputation; don't promise anything that you don't know or can't do so that you never offer more than you can realistically or competently provide.

Carmen López Coral Springs, USA

Please provide your profession prior to becoming a Social Media Manager.

I am a Business Administrator by profession, but at the moment am unemployed. I'm located in southern New Jersey, in the United States

Please share some of the strategies and techniques that have helped you to attract customers.

I like to tell people about how I found my first customers. Though living in an area that has 90% English-speaking population, my English was not so good. I set myself the goal of finding a way to overcome this language-barrier fear and said to myself, "I have to be able to go find somewhere where there are other Hispanic people." Only 30 minutes away from here was Atlantic City.

I had seen an advertisement on a Hispanic channel and thought to myself, "if these people are advertising, it must be because they started their own business." I did a study on the market and saw a great opportunity. I prepared very well, packed my bag with my laptop, wrote up a cover letter explaining the services I had in mind, and went to the restaurant meeting. Although I was unable to succeed on this first attempt, it gave me strength to go to the second meeting, at "La Pancita Rico Sazón," and I successfully closed the deal.

All you have to do is take action. You will feel safe because this book explains very well what needs to be done. And, if you practice enough, you are sure to close your first sale.

As for techniques on finding new customers, here are the

four strategies I use:

- Identify new businesses in my area.
- Offer a demo video.
- Negotiate discounts.
- Give away customized Facebook pages.

Tell us what services and prices you have set for each of the services you perform?

Is it a flat rate or a custom rate for each customer. Here is a summary of various services I provide:

- Creating a Facebook page - Landing Page design with an 'I like' button and an application to download coupons. Content management and responses to comments and monthly statistics. The above is US$200 to US$400.

- YouTube channel creation and management - Creating and editing videos (4 per month). Optimization with keywords and analysis of statistics.

    The fee for this package is normally $300 to $500 and in some cases I can negotiate special rates.

a) **What do you tell the customers so they can understand that they need to include their company in the social networks? b) How do you start business**

with the customers (showing a video, providing a dossier..?)

I talk about the importance of positioning a personal brand on the Internet and within the various social networks. I provide some examples of large companies that are doing it and explain the important reasons for why it's necessary to succeed in the current market - including easier customer communication, inevitably boosting their brand.

I also tell them about a visit to one of my first customers, a Latin restaurant: I got there, showed my business card, and said, "I want to talk to the owner of the restaurant." They informed me that she was not there at that time, but that her daughter was.

So, I took the opportunity to get to know her as well; I asked her age, her name, how the business had been faring, etc. When the owner finally came to speak with me, I had a lot of information already. I asked her how she liked social media marketing, and I explained everything in detail.

She responded, "look, we, my husband and I, own this restaurant. We know that today a presence on the Internet is very important, and I really like what you're telling me." I told them important things about video marketing, Facebook. All we discussed were general terms and we didn't close the deal that day. She said that she had to consult with her husband and I asked, "What if I were to do a sample video and then send it to you by email?" She liked this idea and so I made the video, interviewed her daughter, and emailed the sample video. She was fascinated, and especially receptive to how the video showed them, as they really are - a large advantage of video marketing over Facebook because it attracts all local businesses owners.

Do you do the job yourself, or do you outsource or delegate work to other people?

I perform the main work and delegate graphic design. For example, I have a person who makes the landing pages on Facebook. It works because, personally, I have no experience in graphic design. I highly recommend to everyone that they start off by outsourcing most tasks like design, to allow for more personal time to focus on customers, spend time with your family, and do the things you like.

How has your life changed since you became Social Media Manager?

It has been a 180-degree change. I mean, it has completely changed my life. I have a very well ranked profession as Social Media Manager, I can help businesses and entrepreneurs, I have acquired many colleague friends, I feel fulfilled, and I also see great opportunities for the future as the social media business continues to grow.

I am very happy; this has changed me, it has transformed my life. I have started to realize my dream as business owner. My advice is to just start - put your plans into action, stop being afraid and go! Clients are waiting, they need your help, they need all of the knowledge you have gained in this book.

What are some specific strategies that have helped your business grow?

It is good to have a mentor who can guide you in taking the right action. Also, having an active presence in the various social networks where you can help others. Giving away web presence analysis with business statistics so that they can get a real glimpse of potential business opportunities and gain confidence. The Facebook Ads are also important for helping customers get end customers, but also for me to get my first customers.

What would you say are some of the key qualities to be a successful Social Media Manager?

I have three words that I would highlight and recommend everyone to follow:

- Persistence
- Consistency
- Honesty

In your opinion, is there any aspect that you think is more important to highlight in the work of a Social Media Manager?

As a social media professional with a personal brand, you should be able to persuade customers that they need your services; that you have an offer they can't reject. Another aspect is the training and seminars offered to companies.

Your Next Steps

"Do not wait; the time will never be "just right." Start where you stand, and work with whatever tools you may have at your command, and better tools will be found as you go along." Napoleon Hill

I sincerely hope that these strategies and techniques have given you the information, excitement, and courage to take your first steps towards becoming a Social Media Manager.

Even if you won't be starting any Social Media Manager activities any time soon, I hope that these insights will help you see how to achieve success with social media in today's business environment. All in all, most of the strategies shared here can be applied within any business.

My most important recommendation to you is not to wait, but to take action as soon as you can. Don't worry if you don't have all the right tools and knowledge when you start. You will learn and grow as you take action.

Here's to your massive success,

Lasse Rouhiainen

www.smartsocialmedia.biz/vip

Claim Your Bonus Resources for Book Readers Only

I authored this book so that you will gain a solid understanding of how to become a Social Media Manager and avoid the most common pitfalls. However, I know that you probably still have questions, such as:

- What are my first steps to success?
- How do I prepare for launching my business the right way?
- Where can I get further information and inspiration?

That is only natural and so I have given you, a reader of this book, a special opportunity to receive additional bonuses including video tutorials, checklists and templates for FREE at:

www.smartsocialmedia.biz/vip

About the Author

About the author: An international video marketing and social media marketing expert and trainer, Lasse Rouhiainen is a frequent speaker at business schools and universities on the topics of YouTube, Facebook, and social media marketing. He has helped hundreds of small and medium sized companies and entrepreneurs in over 30 countries to promote their businesses online through social media and video marketing. In addition, he has helped 200 people in over 10 countries become successful Social Media Managers.

Contact Lasse at:

www.SmartSocialMedia.biz/vip

Lasse on social media:
www.youtube.com/coachlasse
www.facebook.com/lasserouhiainen
www.twitter.com/lassevideo
www.twitter.com/lasseweb20

Visit the resource page of this book at:
www.smartsocialmedia.biz/vip

Share This Book

If this book has motivated and inspired you, chances are excellent that this is just what some of your friends and colleagues are also seeking. So, do everyone a favor and share this book! You may also share it on Facebook, Twitter, and other social networks.

If you have enjoyed the knowledge I have shared with you, please take a moment to review my book on Amazon. All of your feedback will help make any revisions (or potentially a sequel) even better than the original.

Thank you so much for all of your time and attention. And good luck!

Made in the USA
Charleston, SC
21 December 2012